BUILDING

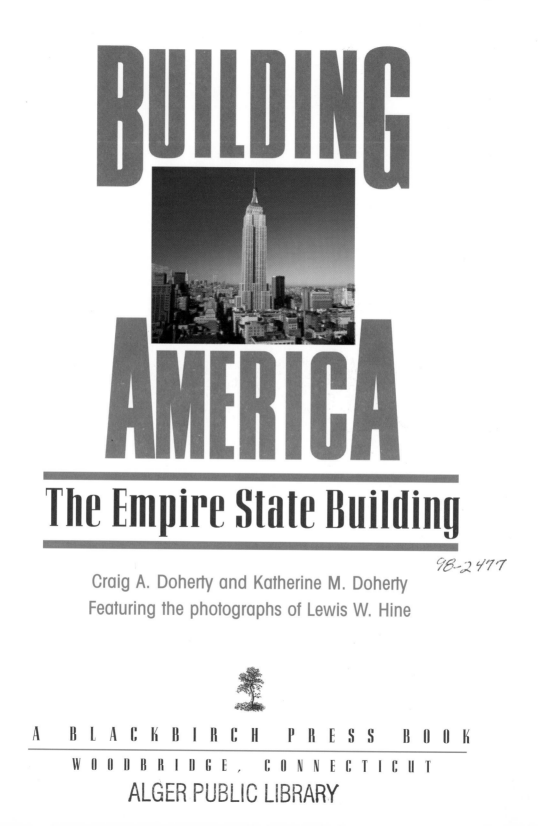

AMERICA

The Empire State Building

Craig A. Doherty and Katherine M. Doherty
Featuring the photographs of Lewis W. Hine

A BLACKBIRCH PRESS BOOK

WOODBRIDGE, CONNECTICUT

To the memory of our friend, Donna Campbell

Special Thanks

The publisher would like to thank Lydia Ruth of the Empire State Building Company for her help in reviewing the material in this book.

Published by Blackbirch Press, Inc.
260 Amity Road
Woodbridge, CT 06525
web site: http://www.blackbirch.com
e-mail: staff@blackbirch.com

Printed in the United States

10 9 8 7 6 5 4 3 2 1

Editorial Director: Bruce Glassman
Senior Editor: Deborah Kops
Editorial Assistants: Laura Norton, Kristina Knobelsdorff
Design and Production: Laura Patchkofsky, Calico Harington

Photo Credits

Cover and page 30 (top): ©Blackbirch Press, Inc.; title page and pages 42–43: ©Rafael Macia/Photo Researchers, Inc.; page 4: ©Jon Hicks/Leo de Wys, Inc.; pages 6, 8, 12, 13, 17, 18 (top and bottom), 19, 20, 22, 23, 24, 25, 26, 28, 29, 32: ©Lewis W. Hine/Romana Javitz Collection, Photography Collection, The Miriam and Ira D. Wallach Division of Art, Prints & Photographs, The New York Public Library; pages 10 (right and left), 16, 36, 37, 38, 39: AP/Wide World Photos; page 14: Culver Pictures, Inc.; pages 30 (bottom), 34: ©Thomas Laird/Peter Arnold, Inc.; page 31: National Archives; page 41: Photofest; page 44: ©Karen McCunnall/Leo de Wys, Inc.

Library of Congress Cataloging-in-Publication Data

Doherty, Craig A.
   The Empire State Building / by Craig A. Doherty and Katherine M. Doherty.
      p. cm.—(Building America)
   Includes bibliographical references and index.
   Summary: Describes the history of the Empire State Building, emphasizing basic architecture, engineering, and mechanical procedures of construction.
   ISBN 1-56711-116-5 (lib.bdg.)
   1. Empire State Building (New York, N.Y.)—Juvenile literature. 2. New York (N.Y.)—Buildings, structures, etc.—Juvenile literature. [1. Empire State Building (New York, N.Y.) 2. Buildings 3. Skyscrapers I. Doherty, Katherine M. II. Title. III. Series: Doherty, Craig A. Building America.
NA6233.N5E53 1998
725'.2'097471—dc21

96–40483
CIP
AC

Table of Contents

Introduction

When the Empire State Building in New York City was completed in 1931, it was the tallest building in the world. It held that distinction for more than 40 years, until the first of the two World Trade Center towers was built in New York City in 1972. Although it is no longer the world's tallest building, the Empire State remains one of the best-known architectural landmarks of all time. Its design and construction are testaments to the creativity and determination of the people that made the project a reality. Out of the darkest days of the Great Depression in the 1930s came one of the greatest structures ever built by humans. It still stands as an enduring symbol of our ability to dream, as well as our ability to realize those dreams.

Opposite:
The Empire State Building remains one of the most famous buildings in the world.

5

Two men named John J. Raskob and Alfred E. Smith were the idea people behind the Empire State Building. (The building's name comes from one of New York State's common nicknames: the "Empire State.") Raskob was a bookkeeper who had worked his way up to the vice-president's office at General Motors. Smith was a charismatic former governor of New York and unsuccessful presidential candidate. Together, Raskob and Smith dreamed of building a "showpiece" that would be higher than the Chrysler Building—which was under construction in New York City at the time—and would briefly hold the position of world's tallest structure.

Once the two men had the idea to build an "Empire State Building," they had to find a suitable place for the structure. Tall buildings and skyscrapers require the support of bedrock underneath them. This is a strong, deep rock that is sturdy enough to hold enormous weight and pressure. Because enough bedrock to support a tall building is only present on Manhattan's southern tip and in the island's midsection, Raskob and Smith's choices were a bit limited. They looked around the city for a suitable location and finally decided that the site occupied by the old Waldorf-Astoria Hotel on Fifth Avenue between 33rd and 34th streets would be the perfect location for their dream building. The two partners specifically wanted a place that would attract businesses because the Empire State Building was slated to be primarily an office rental property. Raskob paid around $20 million for the closed hotel, which was torn down to make way for the new project.

Opposite:
A view from atop early construction in 1931. The Chrysler Building can be seen towering in the background.

1

Dreams of Scraping the Sky

For many centuries, buildings were built so that the walls supported the weight of the structure. The taller and heavier the building, the thicker the walls would have to be to support it. Structures were also limited by the number of stairs it was practical to climb. Many architects and designers felt that more than five or six flights of stairs would be too many. By the early 1930s, two technological innovations changed all these design limitations.

Birth of a Safe Elevator

The first innovation was the development of the Otis elevator. An elevator is simply a box that is suspended by ropes or cables in which people and objects

Opposite:
Two workers inspect parts of the steel frame high above the city.

9

Two Men with a Dream

John Raskob and Alfred Emanuel Smith came from different ends of New York State, and rose to power by very different routes. Raskob was born in Lockport, in upstate New York, in 1879. At the age of 21, he went to work as a bookkeeper for Pierre S. du Pont. Al Smith, whose family had emigrated from Ireland, was born in 1873 in a tenement in Brooklyn. Smith's break came when he got a political appointment from some local officials as a subpoena server. From there, he won election to the New York State Assembly in 1903, and

Al Smith

John Raskob

then became governor of New York. His political career, which seemed limitless, ended one step short of the White House.

While Smith worked his way up through the national political system to become the Democratic presidential candidate in 1928, Raskob was climbing his way to wealth in the business world. Pierre S. du Pont, was one of three du Pont cousins who took over the family chemical and munitions business in 1903. Pierre du Pont became the treasurer and Raskob was named his assistant.

are lifted and lowered. In the early days of elevators, if the supporting rope or cable broke, the elevator plunged to the ground. The first elevators, in fact, were so unsafe that they were only used for freight. In 1853, however, Elisha Graves Otis changed all that. The Otis elevator incorporated a number of safety features, including a set of iron rails inside the shaft, with brakes on the rails. If the cable broke and the elevator began to fall, the brakes would stop the elevator from going into free fall. With safe elevators available, designers and architects were now free from the limitations of staircase-only buildings.

In this position, Raskob often advised du Pont on investment matters. After World War I, du Pont's company had large amounts of cash to invest and Raskob convinced du Pont to invest heavily in General Motors. Du Pont put $50 million into the company and made Raskob a vice-president in charge of GM's finance committee.

It was here that Raskob saw the opportunity to create a new branch of the automotive business. In 1919, Raskob created the General Motors Acceptance Corporation. GMAC's role was to provide financing for individuals who wished to purchase a vehicle from a General Motors–affiliated dealership. This idea was so successful that in less then 10 years, 60 percent of all new vehicles were being bought with GMAC loans. General Motors thus became one of the most successful companies in the world.

Raskob and Smith came from different worlds, and at one time even belonged to opposing political parties. In 1928, however, they found a cause that united them. When Al Smith was nominated to be the Democratic presidential candidate, the repeal of the Eighteenth Amendment was one of his primary objectives. The amendment made it illegal to manufacture or sell alcoholic beverages.

Raskob agreed with Smith on the Eighteenth Amendment issue. With the urging of du Pont, Raskob switched parties and became Al Smith's campaign manager and chairman of the Democratic National Committee. It was at this point in their careers that the two men formed the bond that would eventually lead them to build the world's tallest building together.

The Beauty of Iron and Steel

The other problem that had limited architects in the past was addressed by the greater availability and use of iron. With iron, architects and engineers were able to build a skeleton inside a building to support the weight of a structure. By the beginning of the 20th century, buildings of 20, 30, even 50 stories were being built in cities around the world. But they were still not high enough. Booming city populations created great demand for living and working space. This, in turn, created an even greater demand for bigger—and taller—structures.

When engineers eventually replaced iron girders with lighter but stronger steel, they were able to reach remarkable new heights. The architects at Shreve, Lamb, and Harmon were eager to test the limits of steel girders with new designs. They were given the job of designing the Empire State Building. Raskob made it clear that he wanted them to go as high as the budget would allow.

As the designers worked on their plans, a wonderful design began to take shape. They struggled with a number of the technical details, and presented over 16 different versions of the design before they finally got approval from Raskob, Smith, and the other people involved in the project.

The final plans called for most of the five-story base to be taken up with a grand entrance. The entrance is four stories high with the main lobby inside rising three stories. After the fifth floor, a number of setbacks ("steps" in the contour) begin. The sixth floor is set back 60 feet from the edge below, and a series of setbacks continue to gently reduce

Workers hoist a large steel beam during construction in 1930.

the size of the tower as it rises toward the sky.

After the 80th floor, the tower narrows until it reaches the top-most point—1,250 feet above Fifth Avenue. The tower is then topped with a TV antenna, which gives the structure a total height of 1,454 feet. Observation decks with spectacular views were built on the 85th and 102nd floors. Today, one of the most-visited sites in all of the world is the top of the Empire State Building.

A worker holds materials in place by pulling on a rope.

Perhaps the greatest accomplishment of the design team was the fact that the building was designed to be built both rapidly and easily. This was done by applying the basic principles of the assembly line to the construction process. Most of the necessary parts were fabricated off site, and then brought to the job in the order in which they were needed. Delivery of these materials followed an exacting schedule that enabled the workers at the site to assemble the building like a giant toy erector set.

A final step, before construction, was to have a model of the building made out of plaster. This model of the Empire State Building was 7 feet tall and weighed over 525 pounds. It was so realistic that the Fox Film Company used it instead of the real building when they shot the early talking movie *Skyline*.

2

Into the Bedrock

Before the foundation could be dug, the old Waldorf-Astoria Hotel had to come down. That meant 2,000 tons of iron, 13,000 tons of steel, and tons of other material had to be taken apart and removed from the site. Some materials were sold as scrap, and some of the architecturally unique elements of the old hotel were auctioned off. What couldn't be salvaged or saved was hauled out into the ocean by barge, and dumped about 15 miles beyond Sandy Hook, New Jersey.

Much of the hotel's demolition was done by special workers, who were referred to as "the morticians of the building trade." The most respected of these

Opposite:
The old Waldorf-Astoria Hotel at Fifth Avenue and 34th Street.

15

workers were called "barmen" because they worked with crowbars, tearing apart the building by hand. It was dangerous work that required a good knowledge of how structures were put together. A careless barman could have a section of wall fall on him or have the floor give out underneath him. The demolition of the hotel was completed in January 1930, with a final cost of about $900,000. By the beginning of March 1930, a total of 28,529 truckloads of debris had been removed from the site.

Digging Down to Build Up

With the old hotel gone, 600 workers started immediately on the Empire State Building. The first step in building a skyscraper is to dig down and attach its base to solid rock. One of the reasons that New York City is the location of so many skyscrapers is that the underlying geology of much of the island is solid. Geologists call the layer of rock under the city "Manhattan schist." It is made up of igneous rock that was formed millions of years ago from the molten core of the earth. The workers on this project hit this solid bedrock at only 38 feet down. Two feet of rock was removed to provide a level and relatively smooth surface on which to build.

Al Smith (center) laid the cornerstone for the building in a ceremony in 1930.

Pier holes were then blasted out of the solid rock. Each pier hole was used to anchor a footing for one of the 210 steel columns that would rise out of the ground and support the steel skeleton of the building. Twelve of these columns ran all the way to the top of the building. As soon as half the footings were completed, the steel workers began attaching the columns. The heaviest steel was used at the bottom of the building, where the weight and pressure loads would be greatest. The largest steel beams were called "box columns," and each was designed to support over 5,000 tons of stress. These beams were so massive that they weighed about one ton per foot of length. The average car today weighs less than a ton.

Once the footings were in place, workers began to attach the columns to one another.

Above:
A *worker checks a steel column for straightness ("plumb")*.
Below:
Cranes hoist steel at about 11 stories high.

Up, Up to the Sky

Once the steel started to go up, the assembly-line plan for the construction of the building went into full swing. Steel shipped from Pittsburgh arrived at a special staging yard in Bayonne, New Jersey. There, it was arranged and marked as to its location in the framework, and the number of the crane that was to be used to lift it into place. The steel was manufactured to exact measurements—it could be no more than an eighth of an inch off. Much of the steel became part of the building only 80 hours after it had come out of the blast furnaces of American Bridge and McClintock-Marshall in Pittsburgh!

With this kind of organization and precision, it is no wonder that the project went up with unbelievable speed. The first steel arrived at the site on March 17, 1930. On November 21, 1930, the mast at the top of the tower was in place. Construction averaged about about four and a half stories a week. The erection of such a tall building in such a short period of time was proof that the architects and engineers had planned the unique project with amazing care and precision.

Every aspect and detail of the construction was planned to maximize speed. One of the greatest time-savers was the use of a hand-powered narrow-gauge railroad system. This system allowed workers to move large quantities of materials with ease

to any location on the building during construction. It consisted of 48 specially designed cars. Half were designed to dump their loads. Each of the "dump cars" held 21 cubic feet of materials, which would fill eight wheelbarrows. The other 24 cars were equipped with platforms on which materials could be stacked.

A special construction elevator lifted the loaded cars to the floor where they were needed. From there, a series of tracks led to every work station on that level. Moving materials quickly and efficiently saved time, but it also saved money. With the use of the railway, fewer people were needed to transport supplies to the workers, which in turn greatly reduced labor costs.

Steel is unloaded from a truck as it arrives from the factory in Pittsburgh, Pennsylvania.

Thousands of Rivets

One of the most critical supplies that the railway delivered to the workers was rivets. As many as 100,000 red hot rivets were used to fasten the steel

beams of the Empire State Building together. Rivets look like thick bolts—the end of a rivet is hammered back to secure it in place. At any given time during the construction, 35 to 40 crews of riveters were busy setting rivets.

A riveting gang consisted of four workers. The first was called the "heater" or "passer." It was this person's job to put the rivets in the forge, or furnace, and heat them until they were red hot. The heated rivets were then removed from the fire with 3-foot-long tongs and tossed to the next person in the team. It was not unusual for a heater to toss a rivet 50 to 70 feet up in the air to a higher level on the structure. (It is easier to toss upward than it is to throw to someone on the same level.)

The next worker, called the "catcher," caught the glowing rivet in a tin bucket. The catcher removed the rivet from the can with tongs, and then set it in the pre-drilled holes in the two pieces of steel that were being joined. It was then that the "bucker-up" and the riveter took over.

The bucker-up held the hot rivet in place while the riveter worked a 3-foot-long air-powered hammer, called a jackhammer, that generated 100 pounds of pressure per square inch. Sparks would fly as the end of the rivet was flattened to keep it in place. The heat generated by the glowing rivet—and the force of the hammer—fused the rivets to the steel beams. The noise created by the riveting hammers was so loud that they were only allowed to run between 6 AM and 11 PM. The best riveting gangs could drive over 500 rivets a day during their seven-and-a-half-hour shift. Many

Opposite:
Two workers secure one of the 100,000 rivets used to fasten the building together.

A *"bucker-up" and riveter work on attaching a rivet. The "catcher" (left) stands with his tongs and pail in hand.*

riveters also worked at the highest and most dangerous positions on the steel framework.

As the building climbed toward the sky, an increased number of rivets per square inch were needed to make the building strong enough to stand up to greater forces of wind. (It is not unusual for the building to sway a quarter inch or more, but the greatest movement was recorded during a hurricane in 1938. During this storm—which had sustained winds of up to 120 miles per hour—the building moved as much as 4 inches off center!)

A Layer of Limestone

After the riveters had the steel hammered into place, the other workers came along right behind them. Plumbers, electricans, brick masons, stone masons, carpenters, and a host of other workers all had special jobs to do. And all were expected to meet the demanding schedules of the engineers.

Finishing the exterior of the building was another victory of careful planning. The outside of the Empire State Building is finished in limestone that came from the Indiana Limestone Company. To save time and money, the architects had the stone "rough-cut" at the quarry. It was then sent to New York-area stone workers to have it milled into its final shape and finish. This made it possible to have most of the stone nearby without having to find a place to store it. The local stone workers held it until it was time to deliver it to the building site.

After only a few months of construction, the building stood more than 16 stories high.

The engineers even wrote specifications for the stone so that it could be handled quickly and efficiently. The stone was cut in small enough pieces to be handled by fairly lightweight electric cranes and the industrial railway system. As the stone arrived at the site, it would be loaded on to one of the 24 platform cars. It was then sent up through the center of the building, and rolled along the rails to almost the exact spot where it would be added to the outside of the building. This eliminated the need for lots of exterior cranes that were slower and more dangerous than the rail system.

Workers enjoy lunch on one of the partially completed floors in 1931.

When the stone work was completed, the windows were installed floor by floor. At the same time, plumbers and electricians were busy at work. They would begin work practically before the cement floors were dry. As soon as they were done, the plasterers and woodworkers would move in. They were followed by the painters. The floors of the upper levels sealed the levels below from the weather, so the finish work didn't have to wait for a roof. The lower floors of the building were actually completed while the steel was still being erected on the upper levels! By early 1931, if everyone kept to their schedules, it looked as if the tallest building in the world would be completed in record-breaking time. There was, however, a price to be paid for the speed with which the Empire State Building was built.

Sparks fly as a worker cuts steel with a torch.

The Price of Speed

When people rush to do anything, they make mistakes. The emphasis on speed during the construction of the Empire State Building may have been the primary cause of a number of accidents, and some of these were fatal. Some reports say that as many as 14 people died while working on the project. At the time of the construction, there were rumors that as many as 100 people died during construction, but that was not true.

At least one person was killed by a truck. Another was struck by a hoist used to lift steel. Flaws in the design of safety gates on the construction elevators resulted in another death.

Opposite:
A *steel support is bolted to the frame near the top of the building.*

Some workers put themselves in great danger while on the project. This man is scaling a cable high above the city with no safety equipment.

Nothing, however—not even death—slowed the pace of construction. In one 10-day period, 14½ stories were erected, and that included the steel, concrete, and stone. One of the designers referred to the construction as a "giant parade" with all the marchers keeping step. It was, indeed, a giant assembly line that climbed to the sky.

A Dazzling Exterior

The exterior of the Empire State Building consists of three major components: stone, brick, and glass. The principles of the assembly line were also applied to the bricklayers. Special covered scaffoldings, or platforms, were suspended on the outside of the building. Helpers piled the bricks on the scaffolding so they were always within reach of the masons. Other helpers made sure there was plenty of mortar. The bricklayers barely had to move as brick after brick was placed with amazing speed and accuracy.

When the brick and stone work was completed on a floor, the window frames, glass, and finish work was done. The windows were designed especially for the building and added to

Steel is bolted together. Many workers climbed the heights and worked on platforms with no harnesses or nets.

its sleekness. The window frames were designed to grab attention, as they were painted tomato-soup red.

The tower and observation deck at the top of the building were designed in the Art Deco style. Art Deco reached the height of its popularity in the 1930s. This style was characterized by geometric forms, modern materials, and often, bright colors. The Art Deco top was intended to serve as a mooring for blimp-like aircraft called "dirigibles."

One small, privately owned dirigible made two attempts to deliver newspapers via the mooring, and, although the second attempt succeeded, the mooring was abandoned. It was determined that it would not be safe for a large passenger dirigible to load and unload passengers that high in the air.

Extra-Fast Elevators

One of the most difficult engineering problems inside the Empire State Building was the elevators. The speed of travel was of great importance. The designers ordered elevators that moved cars up and down at speeds of 1,200 feet per minute, but the city building codes only allowed a maximum speed of 700 feet per minute. Designers and engineers appealed the building code restriction, and fortunately, the rule was changed in time for the faster elevators to remain.

THE GREAT CRASH OF 1929

In the 10 years following the end of World War I (1919–1929), the United States experienced a time of great growth and prosperity. The economy grew rapidly and "stock market fever" swept the nation. Many people invested all their savings in stocks that seemed like "sure winners." Many of these investors even borrowed money to buy stocks.

In 1929, the joyride of rising stocks came to a crashing halt. On Tuesday, October 29, the stock market had the worst day in its history. By the end of the year, stocks had lost over $10 billion in total value. Many investors could not pay back the money they had borrowed and were wiped out financially. People began to lose their homes and businesses as economic hard times quickly spread throughout the country, and then the world.

Unemployed men stand in line for a soup kitchen during the Depression.

Ten million workers lost their jobs, and hundreds of banks were forced to close their doors. In the 1932 presidential elections, the country voted overwhelmingly for Franklin Delano Roosevelt and his sweeping New Deal policies that promised to get America's economy back on its feet. It would take another eight years, however—and the economic boost from World War II—to finally put most Americans back to work.

A Multi-ethnic Workforce

At the time the landmark building was built, New York City was truly a multi-ethnic city, as it remains today. The thousands of workers who were employed in the demolition of the Waldorf-Astoria Hotel and in the construction of the Empire State Building project

Opposite top and bottom: Typical Art Deco details—especially geometric shapes—adorn the Empire State Building.

reflected the rich mix of cultures present in the city. As many as 6,000 different workers—representing almost all of the ethnic groups living in the metropolitan area at the time—received paychecks from companies involved in making the Empire State Building a reality.

At the peak of activity, around 3,000 workers were employed at once. This included a number of skilled and unskilled workers. Master electricians ran hundreds of miles of wire, while the plumbers and their helpers put in almost as many miles of pipe. Vents and heating ducts were put in by specialists. Brick masons, ironworkers, derrick operators, carpenters, and elevator installers were all needed to perform their specialties. Every group of workers had their own foreman, supervisors, inspectors, and clerks who kept track of every aspect of the construction. The job even employed young people whose only job was to go around with watering cans to keep the wooden floor planks damp. This kept the dust down on the job. All of these workers combined spent approximately 7 million hours putting together the Empire State Building.

Ironically, for most workers, the reward for building the world's tallest building in record time was not fame or success, but unemployment. By 1931, the Depression had reached near rock bottom. While the Empire State Building was rising high, the number of construction jobs in New York City dropped by 50 percent. As a result, in 1931, many of the workers went from full employment to the relief lines. After their relief ran out, they too would end up in the bread lines.

Opposite: Machinery repair was a full-time job for many workers at the building site.

Instant Celebrity

Dismal economic times presented new problems for the Empire State Building once it was finished. After spending $40,948,900 on the land and construction, Raskob, Smith, and the others involved in the project were faced with the problem of finding tenants. The terrible economic uncertainty of the Depression, however, made renters hard to find. When the building opened on May 1, 1931, it had only 23 percent of its space leased out. Raskob and Smith called on friends and companies involved in the construction to rent space. U.S. Steel rented a floor, as did Starrett Brothers, the general contractor on the project. Du Pont, the company for which Raskob had

Opposite:
As soon as it was opened in 1931, the Empire State Building became one of New York's most popular tourist attractions.

35

worked, leased the 9th, 10th, and 11th floors. By December 1931, with less than one quarter of the Empire State Building's floors rented, some in the business community referred to it as the "empty state building."

By 1936, the situation grew so bad that the building was actually on the verge of bankruptcy. Metropolitan Life Insurance Company, which held the mortgage, reduced the interest from 6 percent to 3 percent to help the management company pay its debt. At one point, Met Life agreed to reduce the interest rate to 2½ percent in exchange for a $500,000 payment on the principal. By 1940, the building was still not generating enough income to cover its 2½ percent mortgage interest payment.

Despite the problems of renting the space, the Empire State Building was a huge success with tourists. The first day the building was open, a total 5,108 visitors paid to travel to the observation level. In the first 34 days, there were 96,109 visitors who had seen the view from the top of the world's tallest building. By the end of the first year, a total of 775,000 people had paid to ride to the top. These tourists also spent more than $875,000 on souvenirs, food, and admissions. This was the only aspect of the project that made any money in the early years.

Hundreds of Employees

Keeping the Empire State Building operational required a workforce of 350 service employees. Two hundred of these workers were required just to keep the building clean inside and out. In the early 1930s and 1940s, one of the most dangerous jobs in the entire city was that of washing windows on skyscrapers. Every window in the building had to be washed about once every two weeks. To accomplish this, eight full-time window washers worked in four teams. Originally, they had worked solo—then one of the washers locked himself out and had to break a window to get back into the building. Window washers used only water, rags, a chamois (drying towel), and an 18-inch squeegee. Rings on the sides of each window enabled the washers to safely hook their heavy leather safety straps. It takes an experienced washer about four minutes to clean a window. Each team could do about 75 windows a day.

In addition to window washers, the building had its own police force, fire and sanitation engineers, plumbers, nurses, painters, and numerous other workers. There was also a post office in the building.

Decorative Art Deco inlays, murals, and sculptures are part of the building's impressive interior.

DISASTER IN THE AIR

Colonel William F. Smith Jr. survived 34 combat missions during World War II only to return home to die in a tragic accident. On July 28, 1945, he was trying to fly into New York City in a 10-ton B-25 bomber. The Empire State Building was one of the visual landmarks that pilots used at the time to get their bearings. On this day, however, the clouds and fog obscured it.

Firefighters inspect the wreckage inside the building.

When Colonel Smith tried to drop down below the clouds to figure out his location, he found himself flying amongst the buildings of the city. Then he found himself flying straight at the famous building at 350 Fifth Avenue. Quickly, he pulled up and banked to the west. The plane climbed rapidly, but not rapidly enough. The B-25 crashed directly into the north wall, hitting the 78th and 79th floors. The hole created by the collision was 18 feet wide and 20 feet high. One engine went completely through the building, out the other side, and landed in the penthouse of a neighboring building. The other engine went into an elevator shaft and ended up in the subbasement with the elevator car that had been somewhere around the 35th floor at the time of the accident.

The mail was collected through special chutes that had been included in the construction. The chutes were specially designed to slow falling packages and envelopes at the 65th and 28th floors. The fear was that friction would ignite the paper if the mail was allowed to free fall for nearly 100 stories!

Numerous businesses in the building supplied many of the needs of the offices. One of the most

The damage caused by the impact was terrible, but most damaging was the fireball created by the fuel that came spewing out of the plane. Sheets of flame coated the building's exterior down to the 65th floor. Even worse was the explosion the fuel created inside the building. Many of the interior walls on the 78th and 79th floors were completely destroyed.

Fortunately, the disaster occurred on a weekend. Instead of the usual 20,000 people being in the building, there were only about 1,500. Eleven people in the building and all three of the plane crew died. Twenty-five others were injured. Had this happened on a weekday, the death toll would most probably have been in the thousands.

The crash occurred at 9:49 AM and, within eight minutes, four fire alarms had sounded. A total of 41 pieces of fire equipment, from 23 different fire companies sped to the scene to fight what was—at the time—the world's highest fire. Somehow, the firefighters were able to contain the blaze between the 75th and 79th floors. There was smoke damage to the floors above.

This hole was left in the north side of the building at the 78th and 79th floors.

The day after the crash, the clean-up began. Amazingly, by Monday morning, the lower floors were open for business as usual. It would take $1 million and a year of work to repair the floors that were affected the most. When engineers and architects examined the building, they were relieved to find that there was no structural damage. Incredibly, their design had withstood a test that no one would have imagined possible.

popular businesses was the Empire State Pharmacy, which had a 113-foot-long lunch counter and took reservations for seats. For those who weren't interested in rubbing elbows with the masses at the lunch counter, there was the 27,000-square-foot Empire State Club on the 21st floor. This was a private social club with several dining rooms—Al Smith was its first president.

Colored lights are used to mark holidays and other special occasions.

Facelifts and Renovations

The Empire State Building has changed owners a number of times since John Raskob died in 1950. In 1951, his heirs sold the building for $51 million. Most recently it was sold to a group of Japanese and European investors for $42 million. Over the years, more money has been invested as numerous projects have been completed to modernize and improve the building.

In 1951, air conditioning was added as far up as the 42nd floor, and a 222-foot TV antenna was erected and placed outside, on top. This gave NBC the strongest signal in the city. By the 1960's, nine stations were broadcasting from the top of New York's most famous building, each paying more than $800,000 a year for the right to do so.

Many TV stations shifted their broadcast equipment to the World Trade Center towers in 1972, but as late as 1997, there were still 16 FM radio stations broadcasting from the top of the Empire State Building.

In 1966, the Empire State's elevators were redone. The original elevators required an operator to handle the stopping and starting of each car. The new elevators were fully automatic. The 58 new elevators required 120 miles of new wire cable, 30 miles of rails, 9 million feet of new wire, and 250,000 feet of conduit piping. At the time, this project constituted the largest set of automatic elevators ever installed.

Energy consumption was a primary concern of the owners in the early 1990's, when they undertook a $5.5 million project. All 6,500 windows in the building were replaced to make them more energy

Movie Icon

From the movie *Independence Day* in 1996, back to the original *King Kong* in 1933, the Empire State Building has appeared in over 100 movies. When the moment comes for the aliens to start destroying Earth in *Independence Day*, the White House in Washington goes first, followed by the Empire State Building. Even alien invaders seemed to understand what an important landmark this building is!

It's not just action movies that feature this famous skyscraper. The Empire State Building has been a rendezvous for lovers as well. Tom Hanks and Meg Ryan finally meet at the top in the romantic comedy *Sleepless in Seattle* (1993). Hanks and Ryan are only following in the footsteps of Cary Grant and Deborah Kerr, in *An Affair to Remember* (1957), and Charles Boyer and Irene Dunne in *Love Affair* (1939). In 1994, Warren Beatty and Annette Bening also stayed true to this tradition in their remake of *Love Affair*.

The film that did the most to immortalize the building to moviegoers, however, combined action with a love story. In the 1933 original of *King Kong*, a giant ape is in love with the leading lady, Fay Wray. Kong is captured on a tropical island and is brought back to New York to be put on display. He finally escapes from his captors, but is hunted down by a small army of people and machines. Eventually, the huge ape climbs up the outside of the Empire State Building in a last-ditch effort to reach safety.

The Empire State Building is "destroyed" by aliens in the movie Independence Day.

efficient. It was estimated that these improvements would save close to $1 million a year in heating and electricity costs. Although the building is approaching its 70th year of operation, it continues to stand out as one of the world's greatest construction wonders. Despite its age, the Empire State Building is still considered by many to be the greatest and most beautiful modern building ever built.

The Empire State Building will forever remain one of the most distinctive shapes in New York City's skyline.

WITHDRAWN

INDEX

FURTHER READING

Adams, Barbara Johnston. *New York City*. Morristown, NJ: Silver Burdett Press, 1988.

Clinton, Patrick. *The Story of the Empire State Building*. Chicago: Children's Press, 1987.

Dunn, Andrew. *Skyscrapers*. New York: Thomson Learning, 1993.

Glassman, Bruce. *New York*. Woodbridge, CT: Blackbirch Press, 1991.

Ricciuti, Edward. *America's Top 10 Skyscrapers*. Woodbridge, CT: Blackbirch Press, 1998.

Stewart, G. *New York*. Vero Beach, FL: Rourke, 1989.

SOURCE NOTES

Barron, James. "Flaming Horror on the 79th Floor." *New York Times*, 28 July 1995, p. B1, B4.

"Conquering the Empire." *Newsweek*, 5 May 1986, p. 29.

"Figuring Out the Next Step." *U.S. News & World Report*, 10 Feb. 1992, p. 11.

Gordon, Jennifer A. "Windows Save Empire State Building $948k." *Energy User News*, Nov. 1994, p.1.

Hasset, Bruce. "Fire in the Empire State Building." *Fire Engineering*, Nov. 1990, pp. 50-63.

Hylton, Richard D. "Searching For a Really High-Profile Investment?" *New York Times*, 20 May 1991, p. D1.

Low, Frances. "A Chase Up into the Sky." *American Heritage*, October 1968, pp. 14–20, 80.

"New York Landmark Sets Disabled Access." *Facts on File*, 21 April 1994, p. 284E1.

"A Piece of the Sky." *Time*, 11 Nov. 1991, p. 73.

Tauranac, John. *Essential New York*. New York: Holt, Rinehart and Winston, 1979.

———. *The Empire State Building: The Making of a Landmark*. New York: Scribner, 1995.

"What Would Fay Wray Say?" *New York Times*, 30 March 1995, p. A22.

CHRONOLOGY

1929 August Funding for Empire State Building arranged.

August 29 Al Smith announces plan to build Empire State Building.

September Deadline of May 1, 1931, set as completion date for the project.
Shreve and Lamb hired as architects.

September 29 ESB Corporation rents space in a nearby office building.

October 29 The Stock Market crashes.

November ESB Corp. announces that the building will be 85 stories.

1930 January Demolition of the Waldorf-Astoria completed. Excavation begun and completed. Foundation almost ready.

March 17 (Saint Patrick's Day) First structural steel set in place.

May 26 Steel framework to the 12th floor.

September 9 Al Smith presides over cornerstone and last rivet ceremony.

September 15 Steel to the 86th floor complete.

September 22 Structural steel complete.

October 6 Floor arches completed.

October 17 Exterior metal completed.

November 13 Exterior stone completed.

November 21 Ceremony for completion of the mooring mast tower.

1931 May 1 Official opening-day celebration.

July NBC leases space at the top of the building for an experimental TV broadcast antenna.

1945 July 28 B-25 bomber flies into the north wall of the 78th and 79th floor.

1951 Empire State Building sold by the heirs of John Raskob.

1964 Outside of building lit-up for the first time in honor of the World's Fair.

1966 Elevators replaced with new automatic elevators.

1972 World Trade Center built, and the Empire State Building loses its status as the world's tallest building.

1976 May The 50-millionth visitor rides to the top of the Empire State Building.

1981 50th anniversary of the building celebrated.

GLOSSARY

assembly line An industrial process first used by Henry Ford in the making of cars. The parts and equipment being assembled arrive at a work station in a predetermined sequence, allowing workers to be more efficient.

bedrock The solid rock underlying the loose sediment of the Earth's surface.

building code Laws that govern the building of structures for a town, city, or state.

crane A piece of construction equipment used to lift heavy objects with a cable.

crowbar A heavy metal bar used for prying objects apart.

demolition To tear down; usually used to describe the tearing down of a building.

dirigible A large blimp-like airship kept aloft by helium and propelled by airplane-style engines. These lighter-than-air craft were popular for a brief period in the early 20th century.

fabricate To make something.

footing A reinforced concrete base to which the steel of a building is attached.

foundation The underlying and supporting base of a structure.

geology The study of the earth and its underlying rock structure.

igneous rock Rock formed from the molten center of the Earth that has migrated to or near the surface.

mooring A fixed object that a craft can be attached to.

observation deck The place near the top of tall buildings that allows people to observe the view.

rivet A steel rod with a head at one end. It is heated, inserted into pre-drilled holes in two pieces of steel, and then hammered over to connect the two pieces.

scaffolding Temporary platforms on which workers can stand while they construct various parts of a structure.

setback The floor area of skyscrapers, and other buildings, which often gets smaller as a building gets taller. Each time the floor area is reduced it is called a setback. Setbacks of certain percentages are often dictated by local building codes.

tolerance A strict limit set on sizes and variations of materials used in construction and set by engineers on a project.